Seasonal Poems

R. Lynn Sauls

*From May to Christmas and
from January to Easter*

TEACH Services, Inc.
PUBLISHING
www.TEACHServices.com • (800) 367-1844

World rights reserved. This book or any portion thereof may not be copied or reproduced in any form or manner whatever, except as provided by law, without the written permission of the publisher, except by a reviewer who may quote brief passages in a review.

The author assumes full responsibility for the accuracy of all facts and quotations as cited in this book. The opinions expressed in this book are the author's personal views and interpretations, and do not necessarily reflect those of the publisher.

This book is provided with the understanding that the publisher is not engaged in giving spiritual, legal, medical, or other professional advice. If authoritative advice is needed, the reader should seek the counsel of a competent professional.

Copyright © 2022 R. Lynn Sauls
Copyright © 2022 TEACH Services, Inc.
ISBN-13: 978-1-4796-1372-4 (Paperback)
ISBN-13: 978-1-4796-1373-1 (ePub)
Library of Congress Control Number: 2021921139

Photo: Author, his wife Helen, and three generations of their family, Cherri Sauls, Copyright © 2021 by R. Lynn Sauls.

Unless otherwise noted, all Scriptures are from The Holy Bible, New King James Version. Copyright © 1982 by Thomas Nelson, Inc.

All italics and words in parenthesis within quotations are added by the author.

About the Author

Richard Lynn Sauls was born January 11, 1933, in a peanut-farm cottage thirty miles from Plains, Georgia, and lived in various places in the South until he graduated from Fayetteville, North Carolina, High School.

He earned a BA in Religion from Southern Missionary College (now Southern Adventist University), an MA in English from Vanderbilt University, a PhD in English from the University of Iowa, and completed post graduate work in journalism at Boston University.

Lynn is a member of the College Seventh-day Adventist Church in South Lancaster, Massachusetts, has been an active member of the Adventist Church since his senior year in high school, has served as elder, has spoken in many churches, and has written many published articles, devotions, and poems, receiving several top awards from the Associated Church Press.

He had a forty-three-year career in education, first serving as an elementary and secondary teacher and principal before teaching literature, creative writing, and journalism at several colleges and universities, including Atlantic Union College, Andrews University, and Southern Adventist University.

Lynn enjoys reading and writing poetry. He especially enjoyed discovering the poetry and prose of the religious poet Thomas Traherne when he completed his dissertation on Traherne's *Meditations on the Six Days of Creation*. C. S. Lewis wrote that Traherne's *Centuries of Meditations* is *"almost the most beautiful book"* in English prose. Lynn finds that it is as much poetry as it is prose.

Lynn also enjoyed watching beavers and other wildlife with his wife, Helen, during the changing seasons on Long Pond in Royalston, Massachusetts. Of late, he has enjoyed time with his family, associating with former colleagues and students, and putting together a book of his articles and meditations and this book of seasonal poems.

Recently, Lynn said the five best things that happened to him are giving his heart to Jesus when he was twelve years old, accepting the Adventist message when he was seventeen, attending Southern Missionary College, enjoying a sixty-seven-year marriage with Helen, and seeing their son grow up to make them proud.

Dedication

This book is dedicated to the teachers who helped me find joy in reading poetry, appreciating the out-of-doors, and experiencing the amazing love of Jesus; and also to the last three generations of my family, all of whom are great sources of delight.

Foreword

By Delmer Davis, Professor of English, Emeritus,
Andrews University

Seasonal Poems is a beautifully-arranged collection, organized not just by the seasons but also anchored to the Christian celebrations of Christmas and Easter.

The poems tie specific and striking images from nature and human experience to the rhythm of Christ's life, His birth, death, and resurrection, emphasizing how central these events are to our own continuous need for spiritual hope and renewal.

Contents

About the Author iii
Dedication v
Foreword vi
God's Seasons 9
From May to Christmas 11
    Enlightenment 12
    Application Test 13
    Begonia Stems 14
    Rawback and Bloodybones 15
    The Mole's Prayer 17
    The Tiger's Prayer 18
    Prodigals 19
    Hypocrite's Love Song. 20
    Pragmatism 21
    Like Ezekiel's Wheels 22
    Still Abiding 23
    Skin Colors 24
    Down Coverings 26
    Moveless Autumn Tree 27
    Now, Long Past Youth 28
    Ichthus 30
    Herod and the Great Red Dragon 31
    New Birth 33
    You, Icarus 34
    Once More Christmas 35
    Participation 36
    A Christmas Prayer 38

From January to Easter **39**
    A New Year's Wish 40
    Elms................................... 41
    Foreknowledge.......................... 42
    From January to Spring.................. 46
    Late Winter Verses 47
    Recurrence 48
    Spring Song............................. 49
    Woods Around Long Pond 50
    Three Steps to the Door 52
    Resurrection Meditation.................. 53
    Deterrent 55
    Invitation............................... 56
    Yes.................................... 57
    Second Advent Scriptures................ 58
    Benediction............................. 60
RESPONSES TO LYNN SAULS'
PUBLISHED POEMS **61**

God's Seasons

God made sun and moon to distinguish seasons,
> and day and night.
and we cannot have the fruits of the earth
> but in their seasons;
but God hath made no decree to distinguish the seasons
> of his mercies;
> in paradise the fruits were ripe the first minute,
and in heaven it is always autumn,
> His mercies are ever at their maturity.
God never says, you should have come yesterday;
> He never says, you must come again tomorrow,
but today if you will hear His voice,
> today He will hear you.
He brought light out of darkness,
> not out of lesser light;
He can bring thy summer out of winter,
> though thou have no spring.
All occasions invite His mercies,
> and all times are His seasons.[1]

---

1 Quoted from John Donne's Sermons in *Listen to Love: Reflections on the Seasons of the Year*, edited by Louis M. Savary et al (New York: Regina Press, 1969), p. 347.

From May to Christmas

Enlightenment[2]

Two children looked for fireflies.
One caught one,
The other none.
But both kept right on looking.

---

[2] Richard Lynn Sauls, *Youth's Instructor*, July 10, 1962, p. 4.

Application Test

As I meet this test,
Help me do my best.
If it be not enough,
I'll still be blest.

You have another plan for me.

Begonia Stems

Trying to extend summer,
Gardeners transplant begonias into flowerpots.
Stems heavy with pink blossoms
Briefly droop from root disturbance.
September lushness begins to sink.

Those who know break stems
And make bouquets that live all winter.
What's left of stubs in pots
Force shades of green and pink by Halloween.

Amazing power, that, in begonia stems.

Rawback and Bloodybones

Grandmother prayed and read her Bible every night.

Half obedient we played nice under the chinaberry tree,
In the barn made tunnels under bales of peanut hay,
Scratched the pet hog until she lay down with contented grunts,
And met the rolling store with the nickel Cousin Vester gave each of us
To shut us up that morning after he made us cry.

Then in the long red dust dog days afternoon scorch,
Grandmother on the front porch sipped Kool-Aid®
With Aunt Pearla and Aunt Mittie Mae.
The two of us moved to the backyard shade,
Drawn by the well.

Daring each other on, we raised up on bare toes
And peered over gray oak planks past ferns and moss
Down the dark shaft.
All we could see was our own small faces looking back at us.

We stretched our necks and raised up more,
Wondering whether what we looked for were two monsters,
Or one with a double name like the Sears and Roebuck store.
And whether it was like the same sow's head and bloody spine
We saw on the kitchen shelf last winter at hog killing time.

Fear gripped us, but not so much

As the wish to know gnawed inside our heads

Ever since morning when Grandmother said,

"Now, Dinah, don't you go near the well.

And Lynnie Boy, don't you go near the well.

Rawback and Bloody bones will get you if you don't do what I say.

Play nice now—don't fight—there under the chinaberry tree."

Grandmother had fifteen children. Most of them turned out right.
She prayed and read her Bible every night.

The Mole's Prayer[3]

I like digging
    in my dark tunnel, Lord,
Where grubs and worms squirm,
Where moist brown earth
    and dandelion roots
Slide against my silky coat.
Please let me stay
    in my accustomed place.
I'd rather not feel the breeze
That blows through green leaves.

---

[3] R. Lynn Sauls, *Insight,* November 8, 1977, p. 3. This poem won first prize in the 1977 *Insight* poetry contest.

The Tiger's Prayer

Lord, keep this jungle dark and wide.
It is getting so I have no place to hide
      from my most unkind enemy, man.
May he not find me here.
Neither let him see me in a zoo.
May he not with glittering wand train
      me to sit on stools and
          jump through hoops of fire.
Help me steal silently through the night.
May no light
      reflect from the flame in my eyes.

Prodigals

Canada geese fly north in spring.

But some of them forget where they belong

And stop near Lake Cayuga, New York State,

Tempted by scattered field corn left by harvesters in the fall.

From lake to field and field to lake,

Their calls no longer sound of ecstasy.

Strong diaphragms develop, not from short flights, but long;

Gluttonous bickerings produce no resonant song.

These pilgrims feed on what the swine leave.

That Canada is their home, they do not know.

They do not rise and go.

Hypocrite's Love Song

God, I love you--this I know:
I didn't go to the picture show,
Came to this Your house instead
To drink Your wine and eat Your bread.

Jesus, Jesus, up above,
You are the one I love.
Holy Spirit, Holy Dove,
You are the source of love.

Two, four, six, eight:
Who do I appreciate?
God the Father,
God the Son,
And God the Holy…

> **Blast that Mrs. Spratt.**
> **Can't see the pulpit cause of her hat.**
> **Can't hear the preacher cause of her brat.**

> …And God the Holy Ghost. Amen.

Pragmatism[4]

Concrete sidewalks
Ruler-like
Try to force our paths.

Our well-worn paths
Quite often, though,
Show sidewalks where to go.

---
4   Lynn Sauls, "Pragmatism," *Spectrum*, Winter 1970, p. 33.

Like Ezekiel's Wheels

Like Ezekiel's wheels
We go in circles—
In circles within circles—
We keep coming back

      to home

      to school

      to work

      to full dress

      to nakedness

      to night

      to morning

      to winter

      to spring

      to You,

O Jesus, we keep coming back to You.
Help us find in You eternal Sabbath, eternal Joy.

Still Abiding

Crops can fail because of drought or too much rain.

Plans we think right and proper don't always prosper.

I have seen houses go up in flames.

All sorts of gadgets and appliances wear out or date out—
>with planned obsolescence, faster than they used to.

Clothing goes out of style yearly.

According to most experts, even rivers and oceans,
the air and earth are getting old and wearing out
like a garment.

But Faith, Hope, Love must still abide.

Skin Colors

Tan is beautiful—
    peanut butter tan
    beige
    light, dark, deep,
    olive, pink tan
    pear-yellow tan.

Red is beautiful—
    cinnamon red
    rust red
    auburn
    cordovan.

Brown is beautiful—
    chocolate brown
    mahogany
    copper
    chestnut
    bronze
    sandstone brown.

White is beautiful—
> vanilla white
> ivory
> creamy white
> peachy white.

Black is beautiful—
> licorice black
> charcoal black
> ebony
> coffee black.

Tan and red and brown and white and black.
God made them all. They are beautiful.

Down Coverings

Late October when golden leaves are falling,
Ducks feed at the edge of a cold pond—
Domestic whites and wild mallards,
Male and female, young and old together.
The days bluster cold and damp,
The sky gray, tree limbs swaying.
Unperturbed, the ducks continue feeding,
Their eyes alive and bold.
Thick coats of down preserve them from the cold.

Moveless Autumn Tree[5]

O to be as moveless as a tree that sways
    within an autumn wind all wet with rain.
To stand there, bare arms lifted up, and
    bear its chill and dampness without pain.
To slumber dead to worry, fret, concern
    and yet live on to greet the spring.
To have my roots around some solid rock,
    down deep away from winter's sting.

---

[5] Richard Lynn Sauls, "Moveless Autumn Tree," *The Youth's Instructor,* November 13, 1962, p. 13.

Now, Long Past Youth

Over and over when I was five or six
I dreamed of waking to find
Four large red boxes under a Christmas tree.
One was a box of fireworks,
One a box of clothes,
One was filled with toys and tricks,
The other with things to eat.
The dream was orderly and neat.
I had better watch out
I had better not cry
I had better not pout
Was very fine
When I was five or six.

Now, long past youth,
Each Christmas brings me closer
To letting go the things I want to keep—
The taste of apple cider in the fall,
The leaping up of flames from maple fireplace logs,
The sound of pond ice breaking in the spring,
The feel of rain against the face,
The scent of fresh cut spruce.

Now, Long Past Youth

Hark the herald angels sing
Glory to the newborn king
Life and light to all He brings
Is Christmas truth
Clung to by those past youth.

Ichthus[6]

swimming out of his ocean into Bethlehem's pond
        He put doing our thing first
slipped out of the hands of this world's fisherman
        more than once
primordial urges did not stick to His scales
would not let His mother come between
would not let His brothers come between
would not let the ones He swam around with come between
His ocean was not of this pond
that one called a devil He told where he could go
would not let the holy fish come between

held His demonstration

nothing stopped Him from doing our thing

call Him ichthus

He spent thirty-three years in the belly of Jonah
        and would like to dwell in each of us for
        a good while longer than that

---

6 R. Lynn Sauls, "Ichthus," *Insight,* June 13, 1978, p. 9. *Ichthus* is the Greek word for fish. It was used by Christians in the first century as an acrostic for Jesus—"Jesus Christ, God's Son."

Herod and the Great Red Dragon[7]

    clouts of smyrrhed air swaddling no O little town

    caravans of dunghills floating down east river

    oil slicks from middle orient dumped by three
            hundred thirty-three thousand three ships

    oxide of rare liquid tinsel in bellies of ocean fish

    detergent enzymes foaming out of gold spigots
            into pink sink pools

    deceptive smoke rising through mounds of jingled
            shoverolet christler foeward and nonreturnable jars

    regular suddenness of loading machines and semi-trucks
            joined by multitudes of superjets 500 feet overhead

    3:00 to 11:00 Tee-vee shows for children home from school

    commercials controlling consumer buying habits long
            before and after nadir's raiders

    garlands of concrete-jungle veins meshing as far away
            as Iowa City

    gobbledygook

    verbal false limbs we are not unsubjected to

    language of white and black racism directed against all
            sorts of honkies and colored people

---

7   R. Lynn Sauls, *Insight,* December 28, 1976, p. 24.

>automotive industry General Motors of which has a budget
>>bigger than most of the you-en countries all put together

pushers

watching their flocks by day

waiting
>stood before the woman about to bear a child
>that they might devour Him when she brought Him forth
>>if only

the Child that's born

the Son that's given
>comes now with bright clouds.

New Birth[8]

When Christ was born,
> He did not awake in heaven,
> in His Father's palace,
> with the sea flowing in His veins.

No silent, ordered night that.
His coming was a coming into chaos.

Like Baby Waselesky born last week,
> red and wrinkled in Clinton Hospital,
> He cried and gasped.

Not knowing why barley straws pierce newborn skin,
> He blinked from manger dust.

In time, in time, in time,
> Mary's stories, goats' milk, Galilean hills,
> wood shavings, synagogue scrolls unrolling,
> hyssop's blood-sprinklings, children laughing,
> merchants cursing, the Holy Ghost leading,
> Jerusalem's doctors questioning...

We, too, must be about our Father's business.

---

[8] R. Lynn Sauls, "New Birth," *Insight*, December 20, 1977, p. 15.

You, Icarus

Not by flapping wax-glued wings,
We hoped to find what we were looking for
      by waiting for the Son to fall.

He fell one night into a bed of barley straw.
At once the straw caught fire.

And is burning still.

You can see our shadows on the stable walls.

Once More Christmas

Finals are important sometimes making up one third the grade.

Subjects are important Language of Visual Art Accounting Theory
> Physical Science Computer Programming Intro to Teaching
> Freshman Rhetoric Making the American Nation Foods
> Philosophical Systems Calculus I Advanced Flight Theory
> Intermediate French Elements of Music Parent-Child Nursing
> SCUBA Theology Research Techniques all of them.

To expose students to major areas of knowledge so that they will
> be able to respond both thoughtfully and emotionally to
> experience to evaluate and organize experience and to cope
> with new and changing experience with sensitivity and
> understanding is important.

But that You came, Jesus—this time of year again we are reminded—
> that You came is all important. Nothing matters without.

Lord Jesus, come once more.

Participation

Not only the green tree towering in the living room,

The look-homeward angel looking homeward,

Silent stars on clear and silent December nights,

The silvered complex of symbols on Christmas cards.

Not only these.

But everywhere I look and all I hear and see and think upon reminds me.

Spring and summer and fall, as well as winter, participates me in that birth.

Even the plaster gargoyle grinning on my bookcase,
comical in its
grotesquery, calls to mind midnight mass
at Notre Dame de Paris.

And the pain of a bruised finger caught between two
firewood logs
is participation in newborn flesh pressed against
rough manger wood.

Thank You, Jesus. Thank You.

A Christmas Prayer[9]

Dear Lord,

Please help us to

listen like the shepherds...

rejoice like the angels...

seek like the wise men...

believe like Mary and Joseph...

and live all year long

with the peace, joy, and love

Christ came to give.

Amen.

---

[9] Message on a Christmas card received December 2019 from Marilyn and Betsy Fleming. Dayspring Cards, Siloam Springs, Arkansas 72761, XJH 213.

From January to Easter

A New Year's Wish

To make wise use of time
> without hurrying,
> without tension,
> with calmness of mind.

To be able to say,
> "It is good.
> I'm enjoying the doing.
> I'm enjoying the having done."

Elms

Limber in January's wind,

Maple, oak, and cherry trees sway in the corner woodlot

Awaiting April's resurrection.

Three dozen dead barkless elms
are not swayed by the wind.

The heat of their decay is imperceptible
on this cold January day.

In the fireplace their translation hastens.

Chunks of whitened elm bones smolder into
white smoke, gold flames, and throbbing red coals,

Warding off winter's chill
Until the spring breeze brings warmth.

Foreknowledge[10]

When God made angels
there were great birth pains
great
When God said LET ANGELS BE
He knew all along someday nearly half
    would walk out on Him and
never
come back

When God said LET THERE BE LIGHT
    FIRMAMENT DRY LAND AND SEAS
    AND GRASS SUN MOON AND
    STARS FISH AND FOWL
    AND BEASTS
when God said IT IS GOOD
He must have had some reservations
(there were great birth pains
great)
for God knew all along of deep darkness
    and thunder and clouds and rain and
    fountains of the deep
not to mention hydrogen bombs and
    sulphurous fire

---

10 Lynn Sauls, "Foreknowledge," *These Times,* February 1969, pp. 6–7.

When God the Father said LET US
the Holy Ghost concurred WHY NOT
Likewise the Son
But there were great birth pains
great
for they knew of Cains Jezebels Judases
        all sorts of princes and violent men
        hypocrites and
me

They knew of places like Sodom Bethlehem
        Jerusalem that stonest the prophets
        Gethsemane Golgotha Babylon
        Rome Africa Asia and the Americas
not to mention where I grew up
They knew

They knew
long before angels sang Holy Holy Holy
long before the big brothers and sisters
shouted
long before Adam said Bone of My Bone
They knew

But they went on ahead
it never once crossed their minds not to
go   right   on   with   it

       all   of   it
       all of the great birth pains

Stands to reason
if you wanted angels who were satisfied
    with you
if you wanted angels who were satisfied
    with each other
if you wanted angels who were satisfied
    with themselves
you'd have to make them so glory could
    rise from the inside
So they could be holy wise good and
    satisfied
t h e m s e l v e s
you'd
have to let them
stand   or   fall
all the time hoping
they would stand

The same for angel goes for man
You never know
That child might grow up to be president
    or wind up in the penitentiary

So they went ahead and did it

They went ahead

They went on ahead

They went right on ahead and said

LET BE

for during the great birth pains and
        ever after

great

great

great

were the shouts arising from eternal
        ecstasies

From January to Spring

Thunder in January
smells of lilacs
and June flowers.

Window thermometer registers 6 degrees.
Chickadee sings phee-pheebee, phee-pheebee.
His courting song can't warm the end of January.

Can 20 degrees Fahrenheit and
chickadee's courting song
mark the 14th day of February?

March 20—Window thermometer may register 70 degrees.
This time
chickadee's phee-pheebee
marks the end of winter.

Late Winter Verses

Ice floating on the river
Reflects warm glow
of winter sunset.

Red-winged blackbird
Singing on a bare swamp willow
Waiting for the ice to melt
Wants to see the spring come in.

Across the valley
Winter sun sets behind hills.
Warm glow still on white snow.

Recurrence

In late winter I listen to Vivaldi's "The Four Seasons."

The first of four concertos is "The Spring":

Three violins sing bird songs,

A forest of instruments murmur to west winds,

And then insistent clouds become a short-lived thunderstorm.

Violins sing bird songs again.

Violas bark the bark of watchdogs guarding sheep.

Shepherds dance.

I join their celebration, assured that spring follows winter.

Spring Song

Red-winged blackbird
Singing on a bare swamp willow
Waiting for the ice to melt
Wants to see the spring come in.

Woods Around Long Pond

(Royalston, Massachusetts)

No ghosts of Wampanoags haunt these woods—
Only imaginary echoes of wolf howls
And yowls of cougars in the night.

The other sounds are real—
Wood duck cries,
Bittern calls,
Waters falling over glacial rock,
Mewings of beaver kits,
Chorus of frogs,
Drummings of ruffed grouse,

And the occasional hooting of a barred owl
>	(Who Cooks for You? Who Cooks for You All?).

No arrowhead has ever been found here
Though many in bordering townships
Along with other artifacts of blood and labor.

Did the Wampanoags save this place
For love and contemplation
(NO HUNTING ALLOWED,
NO WARPATHS PERMITTED)
Where braves and squaws could steal away
To watch wood ducks mate
And listen to red-winged blackbirds sing courting songs?

Three Steps to the Door

If no One is to come, no One arose,
No One was crucified, no God walked dusty paths,
No Child went about His father's business,
No Child was born, no Son given,
Matthew, Mark, Luke, and John made up
A right good story.

If no One is to come, no One arose,
But One was sore oppressed,
A Man did walk Judean roads,
A Child went forth, a Son was given,
Behold the Man!
Better to try on His story
Than that of Richard Cory.[11]

He did come, is risen, indeed.
Believe you Him.
God was as human given, wore flesh,
Gave good news to rich and poor.
Bore all our sorrows, will come once more.

Good Grief
Opened up the door.

---
11 Edwin Arlington Robinson, "Richard Corey," Modern *American Poetry*, ed. Louis Untermeyer, 1919, p. 45.

Resurrection Meditation[12]

On this April Sabbath—this holy Saturday—Christ lies buried in our hearts.

While cold rain, mixed with a little snow, falls gently to the waking earth,

> buds are swelling.

Hymns from competing churches sound all right next to each other:

"Amazing Grace" follows Luther's "Mighty Fortress" and a Shaker song.

Then it's silent once again.

A few hours ago we sat in silence trying to have a Quaker meeting.

Christ, from his Roman crucifix, looked on at our discomfort.

Jesus lies buried in our hearts. Tomorrow is the day to celebrate His

Resurrection.

We'll chant and say Episcopal prayers
from the Book of Common Prayer—
an uncommon thing for us, and
at an uncommon hour.

---

[12] Written at an oeccomenical retreat conducted by Atlantic Union College Honors Core on Easter weekend in the 1980s.

May the cold rain cease, the sun shine, the buds open,
the earth awake.

May Jesus rise within our hearts, indeed.
May Jesus Christ be praised.

Deterrent

No assurance
of salvation
needed.
Only this:
God is love.

Should the sun
threaten to blow up,
no crisis to lie awake
nights over.

Should I turn away
and to apparent nothing go,
even then
never once would He forget
time was I loved Him.

Millennia hence
He would lift
scarred hands,
smile,
but also weep.

Invitation[13]

"Come and see,"
The Galilean said
To those who
Asked Him where He lived.
They followed,
And in His house remained.

"Come and see,"
Said Philip to Bartholomew
When doubts his friend expressed.
He went,
And he was satisfied.

"Come and see,"
A woman of Sychar said,
"And I will show you Him,
Who told me everything
I ever did or knew."
They rushed outside the gates
and found the One they had
long been looking for.

---

13 Richard Lynn Sauls, "Invitation," *These Times,* May 1962, p. 1.

Yes

Like Bethlehem's innkeeper,
and King Herod,
and the great red dragon,
I have said *No* to Goodness.

Now I'm tired of No.
Am I ready for Yes?
Yes?   No?   Yes?

YES.
YES. NOW I'M READY.
YES, YES. YES. YES. YES.
YES, JESUS, YES.

Second Advent Scriptures

JOHN 14:1–3

Let not your heart be troubled; you believe in God, believe also in Me.

In My Father's house are many mansions.

If it were not so, I would have told you.

I go to prepare a place for you.

And if I go and prepare a place for you,

I will come again and receive you to Myself;

that where I am there you may be also. JESUS

ACTS 1:9–11

Now when He had spoken these things, while they watched,

He was taken up and a cloud received Him out of their sight.

And while they looked steadfastly toward heaven,

two men stood by them in white apparel, who said,

"Men of Galilee, why do you stand gazing up into heaven?

This same Jesus, who was taken up from you into heaven,

will so come in like manner as you saw Him go into heaven." LUKE

REVELATION 21:1a, 3–4; 22:17, 20

Now I saw a new heaven and a new earth,

for the first heaven and the first earth had passed away.

And I heard a loud voice from heaven saying

"Behold, the tabernacle of God is with men,

and He will dwell with them, and they shall be His people.

God Himself will be with them and be their God.

And God will wipe away every tear from their eyes;

there shall be no more death, nor sorrow, nor crying.

There shall be no more pain,

for the former things have passed away."

And the Spirit and the bride say "Come."

And let him who hears say, "Come."

And let him who thirsts come.

Whoever desires, let him taste of the water of life freely.

He who testifies to these things says, "Surely I am coming quickly."

Amen. Even so, come, Lord Jesus. JOHN

TITUS 2:11–13

For the grace of God that brings salvation has appeared to all men,

teaching us that, denying ungodliness and worldly lusts,

we should live soberly, righteously and godly in the present age,

looking for the blessed hope and glorious appearing

of our great God and Savior Jesus Christ. PAUL

Benediction

Jude 24, 25

Now to Him who is able to keep you
    from stumbling,
And to present you faultless,
Before the presence of His glory with
    everlasting joy,
To God our Savior,
Who alone is wise,
Be glory and majesty,
Dominion and power,
Both now and forever.
Amen.

RESPONSES TO LYNN SAULS' PUBLISHED POEMS

Beautiful. Inspiring. I'm referring to the poem by writer-teacher Lynn Sauls. Clearly, God has not limited psalmist talent to the long-ago days of David.
—Harvey Hanson, Clearwater Lake, Wisconsin

Thanks for the excellent, thought-provoking poem, "Foreknowledge."
—Bob Nixon, former assistant editor, *These Times*

Lynn Sauls succeeds admirably in his application of the modern idiom to an eternal theme.
—Verne Wehtje, Department of English, Union College

I see great artistry and fine craftmanship in Lynn Sauls' poem. The diction is current yet subjectively dignified. The poem helps us begin to feel a glimmer of the immense spreading power of God's love.
This is one of the best poems I have ever seen.
—Wayne Hamm, United States Navy

...preserves the essentials of the gospel while using new and creative approach.
—Victor Griffiths, Department of English, Union College

TEACH Services, Inc.
PUBLISHING

We invite you to view the complete
selection of titles we publish at:
www.TEACHServices.com

We encourage you to write us
with your thoughts about this,
or any other book we publish at:
info@TEACHServices.com

TEACH Services' titles may be purchased in
bulk quantities for educational, fund-raising,
business, or promotional use.
bulksales@TEACHServices.com

Finally, if you are interested in seeing
your own book in print, please contact us at:
publishing@TEACHServices.com

We are happy to review your manuscript at no charge.

www.ingramcontent.com/pod-product-compliance
Lightning Source LLC
Chambersburg PA
CBHW042136160426
43200CB00019B/2953